Set design by Derek McLane

Photo by Joan Marcus

A scene from the New York production of *I am My Own Wife*.

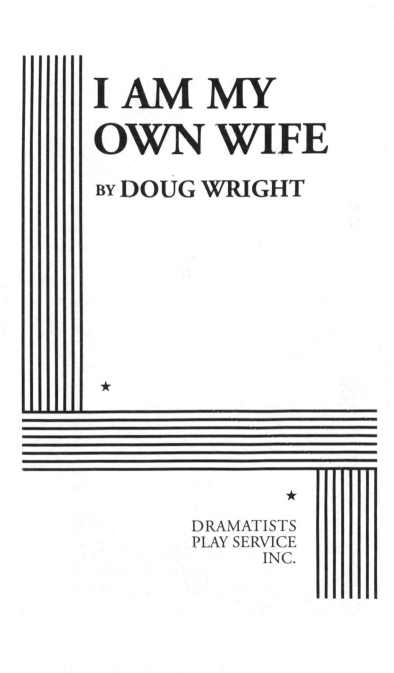

# I AM MY OWN WIFE

BY DOUG WRIGHT

★

★

DRAMATISTS
PLAY SERVICE
INC.

**SPECIAL NOTE**
Anyone receiving permission to produce I AM MY OWN WIFE is required to give credit to the Author as sole and exclusive Author of the Play on the title page of all programs distributed in connection with performances of the Play and in all instances in which the title of the Play appears for purposes of advertising, publicizing or otherwise exploiting the Play and/or a production thereof. The name of the Author must appear on a separate line, in which no other name appears, immediately beneath the title and in size of type equal to 50% of the size of the largest, most prominent letter used for the title of the Play. No person, firm or entity may receive credit larger or more prominent than that accorded the Author. The following acknowledgments must appear on the title page in all programs distributed in connection with performances of the Play:

I AM MY OWN WIFE was originally produced on Broadway
by Delphi Productions and David Richenthal.

Playwrights Horizons, Inc., New York City,
produced the World Premiere Off-Broadway in 2003.

This play was written with support from Playwrights Horizons,
made possible in part by funds granted to the author
through a program sponsored by Amblin Entertainment, Inc.

A workshop of the play was presented by La Jolla Playhouse;
Des McAnuff, Artistic Director, Terrence Dwyer, Managing Director.

Developed in part with the support of the Sundance Theatre Laboratory.

A workshop was also presented by the About Face Theatre
(Eric Rosen, Artistic Director) in association with the Museum of Contemporary Art.

**SPECIAL NOTE ON RECORDING AND SLIDE**
A CD containing recorded text for this play and a slide for post-performance display are required for production and are available for lease through the Play Service for a flat fee of $25.00 and a $25.00 refundable deposit, plus shipping.

*For my four very dedicated "wives":*
*Jefferson Mays, John Marks,*
*Jeffrey Schneider and Moisés Kaufman*

# ACKNOWLEDGMENTS

For their tireless support in bringing Charlotte von Mahlsdorf all the way from East Berlin to the Broadway stage:

Robert Redford, Ken Brecher, Philip Himberg, Robert Blacker and the Sundance Theater Institute, Eric Rosen, Heather Schmucker and the About Face Theater Company in Chicago, Jim Nicola and the New York Theatre Workshop, Des McAnuff, Shirley Fishman, Carrie Ryan and the La Jolla Playhouse, Paul Lister and Dreamworks SKG, The Tectonic Theater Project, Blanka Zizka, Jiri Zizka and the Wilma Theater in Philadelphia, Tim Sanford, William Russo, Sonya Sobieski and Playwrights Horizons in New York, Carol Rigolot and the Council of the Humanities at Princeton University, The German Department of Vassar College, The MacDowell Colony, Yaddo, the staff of *Prinz Eisenherz Buchladen*, Drew Hodges and Spotco, Taylor-Wessig in Berlin, David Richenthal, Sarah Jane Leigh, Doug MacLaren, David Colden, Steve Simons, Marcus MacGregor, Steven Roose, David Schmerler, Kent Eiler, Eva Longscharitsch, Joyce Ketay, Jason Baruch, Richard Kornberg, Sam Cohn, Denise Oswald, Debra Immergut, Christopher Ashley, Andreas Meier, Michael Borowski, Kenny Mellman, Justin Bond, David Hines, Lauren Landau, Mary Hines, Philip Sherwell, Matthew Shiner, James Marion, Allison Rutledge-Parisi, Michael Cadden, Drake Baer, Susan Kittenplan, David Clement, David McDowell, Tom Cole, Olga and Chris Hartwell, Emery Snyder, Kim Benzel, Cynthia Walk, Christopher Murray, Hans Homann, Alan Schrier, Dominic Balletta, Paul Eric Pape, Susan Lyons, Jeff LaHoste, Peggy Wreen, Synthia Rogers, Linda Raya, Anne Poyner, Miss Lillian, the entire Wright family and one used '86 Honda Civic named Madge that was once valued at almost twenty-five hundred bucks.

I AM MY OWN WIFE received its world premiere at Playwrights Horizons (Tim Sanford, Artistic Director; Leslie Marcus, Managing Director; William Russo, General Manager) in New York City, opening on May 27, 2003. It was directed by Moisés Kaufman; the set design was by Derek McLane; the lighting design was by David Lander; the sound design was by Andre J. Pluess and Ben Sussman; the costume design was by Janice Pytel; the translator was Jeff Schneider; the production manager was Christopher Boll; and the production stage manager was Andrea "Spook" Testani. It was performed by Jefferson Mays.

The Playwrights Horizons production of I AM MY OWN WIFE was subsequently produced on Broadway by Delphi Productions (David Richenthal, Anthony D. Marshall, Charlene Marshall) in association with Playwrights Horizons at the Lyceum Theatre, opening on December 3, 2003. After the show opened, Nancy Harrington took over as production stage manager from Andrea "Spook" Testani; the assistant stage manager was Thea Bradshaw Gillies.

# THE CAST

A single actor performs all of the roles in the play. Distinctions between characters are made by changes in the tonal qualities and pitch of the actor's voice; through his stance, his posture, and his repository of gestures. He glides fluidly from one personality to the next. Often, his transformations are accomplished with lightning speed and minimal suggestion; a raised eyebrow or an unexpected smile.

# THE COSTUME

His basic costume is deceptively simple; he wears a black skirt, rimmed with peasant piping at the hem. A black blouse with short sleeves. A black kerchief on his head. Sensible, black walking shoes with scuffed toes. A delicate string of pearls. No make-up.

His clothing is constant throughout most of the play; he rarely uses other costume pieces to represent fellow characters. This is his primary uniform. Every character in *I am My Own Wife* wears a dress by default; transvestism is the norm.

The character of Alfred Kirschner is the one exception to this rule. At the top of Act Two, Alfred appears in an old plaid shirt, wool trousers, and a beret.

The dress designed by Janice Pytel for the original production of *I am My Own Wife* was a marvel of versatility. It had the square shoulders of an officer's uniform, an almost-masculine collar, but delicate pleats which femininely tapered the torso. Without appearing overtly theatrical the dress not only suited Charlotte herself, but also subtly suggested the multitude of other characters included in the play. The over-skirt was full, so the actor could achieve a variety of effects by manipulating it artfully — raising it to marvel in the mirror as an awe-struck young girl; lifting it to curtsy; coyly flipping it back and forth to flirt; and smoothing it with an old woman's modesty when she rises from a chair.

# THE SETTING

A simple, square room, indicated by floorboards and a rear wall, covered in delicate blue-gray lace. In the midst of the wall, a set of white French doors. Onstage, a plinth which will later hold Charlotte's beloved Edison phonograph. A table with four wooden chairs, carved in the neo-Gothic style. Beneath it, a large wooden box. Inside that box, doll furniture, accurately and lovingly carved.

For the original production of *I am My Own Wife*, director Moisés Kaufman, set designer Derek McClane and lighting designer David Lander worked in concert to create a heart-stopping effect on the rear wall of the theater. Looming behind Charlotte's modest quarters was a huge wall of shelving, over-stuffed with antiquities: gilded mirrors, upturned chairs, ornate German cabinetry, porcelain dogs, sideboards, tea tables, music machines of all makes and varieties, old crystal chandeliers, bureaus, bric-a-brac, and bronze busts ... marvelous debris culled from the nineteenth century and hoarded with a kind of obsessive grandeur. At key moments in the text, nine or ten gramophone horns would suddenly erupt in light, revealing themselves for — seemingly — the first time. Other times, twenty clocks would ignite and chime. When Charlotte descended into the famous old cabaret — *die Mulackritze* — countless tiny, fringed lamps with red bulbs sprang to life. The wall gave the play an epic scope; Charlotte's repeated descriptions of furniture became — through visual enhancement — a record of lives lived through the objects left behind. At the same time, this wall was used with such prudence — so judiciously — that visual pyrotechnics were never allowed to upstage the content of Charlotte's own remarkable stories.

These ingenious flourishes belong to the play's original creative team, but I hope they suggest the magical possibilities of Charlotte's world.

# CHARACTERS
(in order of appearance)

CHARLOTTE VON MAHLSDORF
JOHN MARKS
DOUG WRIGHT
TANTE LUISE
SS OFFICER
SS COMMANDER
YOUNG LOTHAR BERFELDE
HERR BERFELDE
PRISON GUARD
MINNA MAHLICH
CULTURAL MINISTER
STASI OFFICIAL
ALFRED KIRSCHNER
YOUNG HOMOSEXUAL MAN
AMERICAN SOLDIER AND HIS BUDDY
CUSTOMS OFFICIAL
STASI AGENT
NURSE
PRISON OFFICIAL
GERMAN NEWS ANCHOR
POLITICIAN MARKUS KAUFMANN
ULRIKE LIPTSCH
JOSEF RUDIGER
ZIGGY FLUß
FIRST NEO-NAZI
SECOND NEO-NAZI
BRIGITTE KLENSCH
KARL HENNING
FRANCOIS GARNIER
SHIRLEY BLACKER
DAISUKE YAMAGISHI
MARK FINLEY
PRADEEP GUPTA
CLIVE TWIMBLEY
DIETER JORGENSEN

# I AM MY OWN WIFE

## ACT ONE

*The French doors at the rear of the room open, and — standing before us — Charlotte von Mahlsdorf. She is, in fact, a man, roughly sixty-five years old. Charlotte wears a simple black house dress with peasant stitching, a kerchief on her head, and an elegant strand of pearls. She gazes at the audience for a moment; the tiniest flicker of a smile dances on her lips. Then — surprisingly — she closes the doors as quickly as she appeared, and is gone. A pause. The stage is empty again. In a moment, the doors re-open. Charlotte re-appears. Cradled in her arms, a huge, antique Edison phonograph complete with an enormous horn in the shape of a flower. She grins, satisfied, and sets the phonograph on a small plinth. She steps back for a moment to admire the music machine. When she speaks, it's in broken English, but the cadences of her voice are delicate; there's a musical lilt to her inflection. She has a German accent.*

## SUPERTITLE: A LECTURE ON THE PHONOGRAPH

CHARLOTTE. Thomas Alva Edison was the inventor of the first talking machine of the world in July of 1877. And you see, the record is not *ein plattenspieler; nein*. It is a cylinder, made of wax. And this record is working with 160 revolutions per minute, and is playing four minutes long. And the record is made by the National Phonograph company in Orange, New Jersey. At one time, I had over *fünfzehntausend* cylinders. *(Charlotte indicates a painting of the Edison phonograph with an attendant dog, its ears cocked to listen:)* And you see — on the wall — a painting: the dog, Nipper, "His Master's Voice." The most famous trademark in all the world. Next month, this phonograph will be half a century old. *(She begins to turn the handle on the phonograph, readying it for play.)* For fifty years, I've been turning its crank.

The loudness depends on a big or a small horn. Metal horns are better for bands and the voices of men, and the wooden horns, they are better for the strings and the voices of the female. *Die Sopranistin.* And Edison's phonograph has in the needle a little sapphire. *(She plucks a tiny, disposable needle from a drawer concealed in the phonograph. She holds it up to the light, and says emphatically:)* *Nicht diamant; nur Sapphir.* And when it grazes the record, it sounds so nice. *(She installs the needle on the arm, then delicately places the arm on the wax cylinder. The machine begins to play; an old German waltz, scratchy and exquisite.)* In the Second World War, when the airplanes flew over Mahlsdorf, and the bombs were coming down, I played British and American records. And I thought, "They can hear in the airplanes that I am playing Edison records." I thought — if they hear me — they will know I'm their friend. *(A pause as Charlotte revels in the music. Then — abruptly — the music stops. Charlotte is supplanted by someone else; a thirty-something news man named John Marks. John has the intrepid spirit of a Saturday serial matinee hero. His voice has a Texas twang. His masculine edge stands in sharp contrast to Charlotte's demure nature.)*


**SUPERTITLE: THE WORLD FLIPS UPSIDE DOWN**


JOHN.  From the desk of John Marks
  Bureau Chief, Berlin
  U.S. News and World Report
  September 1990.
  Dear Doug,
  It's a funhouse over here. You can't imagine. The Berlin Wall falls, and the world flips upside down.
  All the great and powerful leaders are turning out to be clowns. Erich Honecker, one of the most feared and respected dictators in the world, has in one year become a fugitive. He wanders around the grounds of a Soviet Military Hospital in his pajamas. Secret Police files kept on East Germans for four decades are being released, and it turns out husbands spied on their wives, children on their parents, dissidents on each other. *(He steps forward, and*

*adopts a more confidential tone:)* Now in the midst of all this craziness, I've found a true character; she's way up your alley. (And believe me, I use the term "she" loosely.) I'd love to interview her; make her my first official article for *U.S. News and World Report*. But I'm afraid my editor will say her story's too extreme. Still, I think she may well be the most singular, eccentric individual the Cold War ever birthed.

Have I piqued your interest?

Love,

John. *(Another abrupt shift; Doug is a playwright, in his mid-thirties, with an eager-to-please manner and a somewhat mellifluous voice.)*

DOUG. "Piqued" indeed.

August 8, 1992. I've been in Berlin for two days now. I'm sleeping on John's floor. Today we went to the Reichstag; there were demonstrations, because Cristo wants to cover it in pink tulle. Now we're in John's car, headed toward the east. *(Doug glances out an invisible window, as though he were riding in a car with John.)* Through the windshield, I can see fragments of the infamous wall still standing. Slapped onto one in bold paint the words "Art Survives."

A sign whizzes past: "Mahlsdorf." It's a grim place; vast apartment complexes rise like cement gulags. Then we turn a corner, and it's like we've turned back the clock two hundred years or more. Standing before us, a huge, weather-beaten mansion made entirely of stone. About a hundred tourists gathered at the front door. Suddenly — with a creak — it opens — *(Doug morphs into Charlotte. She fingers her pearls. Music from an Edison Amberol wafts through the air.)*

## SUPERTITLE: DAS GRÜNDERZEIT MUSEUM

CHARLOTTE. — *Wilkommen in meinem Gründerzeit-Museum.* Welcome to my Gründerzeit Museum.

Here, people can always come to see my collection. Everything from *die Gründerzeit;* this was the period in Germany between 1890 and 1900. *Wie soll ich sagen ...* "The Gay Nineties." Petroleum lamps and vases, gramophones, records, matchboxes, telephones, ink wells, polyphons, pictures, credenzas, bureaus, and — of course — clocks.

No matter what people want to see or hear, I'll show or play it. Some people, they come to see me. *Ich bin Transvestit.* But soon, they look at the furniture.

*Folgen Sie mir, bitte, ja? (Charlotte pulls the doors of the museum open.)* This old door? It is not original, *nein.* I saved it from a house on Prenzlauer Street. Before the Russians blew up the houses, I took such things. *(As Charlotte enters the museum, Doug addresses the audience directly, recounting the adventurous step into the unknown:)*
DOUG. She ushers us into the foyer of the museum. The ceilings are high; at least fifteen feet. We're huddled together like schoolchildren. For the next two hours — room by room, object by object — she guides us through the house. *(Charlotte seats herself at a small, ornately-carved wooden table. From beneath it, she pulls a velvet jewelry box. She places it squarely in the center of the table. With great ceremony, Charlotte opens it.)*
CHARLOTTE. Come in, please. There is room for everyone, yes? *(Charlotte pulls a small, lovingly carved, elegantly furnished doll dresser from the box. She holds it sweetly in her palm, and approaches the audience, holding it out for inspection.)* Here we have *eine alte Anrichte.* A cupboard, yes? *Und dieses Möbelstück* is made of oak, in the style of Neo Renaissance. But this was not hand-made; this is factory-made. So-called "mass production." And the trim? People would tear it off; they would burn it. They did not like the scalloped wood, the tiny turrets, the ornamental moulding. "Too old-fashioned! Too difficult to dust!" But me ... I had a feeling for such things. And so I saved it. *(She removes a tiny lacquer cabinet of lighter wood.) Und hier haben wir ein Vertiko.* An old sideboard, *ja?* It was designed and built by *ein Tischlermeister,* Otto Vertiko. In *achtzehnhundertfunfundneunzig. (She pulls out a tiny bust on a pedestal:)* And this is a bust of Wilhelm II, the last German Emperor. During the Second World War, they wanted to melt it down for munitions. And so — with my school friend Christian — we pulled it from the bonfire, yes? It looks like a bronze bust, but it is only zinc. Galvanized. Not so expensive. *(Next, a miniature clock with an open, suspended pendulum.)* In French, this clock is called *"regulatour."* Because it is regulating the time. And *auf Deutsch* we say *"Wanduhr," oder "Freischwinger."* Because the pendulum isn't encased in a glass box; it's freely suspended. Of course, American soldiers thought they were nice. They didn't have them in the USA. It made a nice gift to bring to the little wife at home, *ja?*

To wind such a clock, you need a key. And I collected — when I was a child — many keys. Keys for desks. Keys for doors. Keys

12

with no locks; cast-aways. These, I still carry in my apron, *ja? (She extracts a tiny gramophone:)* And here, we have an old gramophone. *Nicht* phonograph; *sondern* gramophone. Instead of cylinders, round plates, flat, *mit* grooves. At one time, I had many such records; Mendelssohn and Offenbach. But during the time of Hitler, it was very dangerous to possess music from Jewish composers. And so I thought, I must save these records. And so I took old paper — brown grocery paper — and I cut it in the shape of labels. And I wrote with ink false titles: Aryan polkas and waltzes, yes? And I glued them onto the records, for safety. And when the war was over, I took a sponge and with water I took the labels back off. And then the Hebrew titles with the dog Nipper were visible again. *(A dainty little kitchen contraption, affixed to the edge of a tiny cutting table:)* The kitchen is like it was for a housewife of 1890 in Berlin. This machine is to pit the stones of cherries. *(She regards the tiny room — now spread out before her on the table, like the parlor in a doll house — for a moment.)* When families died, I became this furniture. When the Jews were deported in the Second World War, I became it. When citizens were burned out of their homes by the Communists, I became it. After the coming of the wall, when the old mansion houses were destroyed to create the people's architecture, I became it. *(A pause, and then:)* I am like a maid-servant in this house; you must clean and clean because the dust is growing! And the dust is looking like the dust of 1890! And you must put it away!

I worked thirteen years with two hands to repair this old house. Each tile on the roof, I know. Each plank of the floor, like an old lover. In August 1993, the collection exists at the museum in this house for thirty-three years. *(She holds up a small collection box:)* And now you may make *eine Spende*. A small contribution. We have a cash box. Each person, what he or she thinks. *(She curtsies, then transforms into Doug.)*


## SUPERTITLE: POPPING THE QUESTION


DOUG.  From the desk of Doug Wright
   New York City
   Dear Charlotte von Mahlsdorf,
   Recently, while in Berlin, I visited your museum. My childhood friend John Marks and I were awestruck by your furniture collec

tion and your astounding array of Edison phonographs.

But I must confess, I was no less impressed by the mere fact of your survival. I grew up gay in the Bible Belt; I can only begin to imagine what it must have been like during the Third Reich.

The Nazis, and then the Communists? It seems to me, you're an impossibility. You shouldn't even exist.

So here's the presumptuous portion of my letter. I would love the opportunity to continue to study your life in order to write a play about you. With your support, I can apply for funding, fly back to Berlin, and begin to write in earnest. As far as grant applications go — forgive me — but from where I sit, you're a slam dunk.

Even if you reject my proposal, please know that the morning you shared with us was one of the most memorable of my life. Thank you for your kind attention, and I look forward to hearing from you.

Sincerely,

Doug Wright. *(Charlotte puts the letter down; she pauses, considering the request.)*

CHARLOTTE. Dear Mr. Wright,

Yes. Perhaps it is possible for you to make a play. Maybe you will visit Berlin after Christmas.

Sincerely,

Charlotte von Mahlsdorf. *(Doug, ecstatic, springs into action, giving the "thumbs up" sign; they're in business now! He circles the stage, reciting into his mini recorder:)*

DOUG. Testing. Testing one-two-three. Testing.

Tape One. It's January 20, 1993. I'm headed to the Gründerzeit Museum in Mahlsdorf for my first official interview with Charlotte von Mahlsdorf. With me, John Marks. *(He sits. On one side — presumably — John Marks. On the other, Charlotte.)*


## SUPERTITLE: TRANSLATING TANTE LUISE


DOUG. John — if you could please — would you ask Charlotte about her given name? Her legal name?

JOHN. *(His Texas twang evident.)* Was war Ihr Geburtsname?

CHARLOTTE. *Mein Geburtsname war Lothar. Lothar Berfelde.*

JOHN. It was Lothar —

⁀OUG. Yeah, yeah. I got that. And next, could you ask her when

she knew ,... the precise time ... that her name ought to be Charlotte?
JOHN. *(Even sharper on the ear this time.)* Und wann wußten Sie,
daß Ihr Name Charlotte hätte sein sollen? *(Charlotte decides to put an
end to this auditory torture.)*
CHARLOTTE.  I can tell it in English, yes? *(John and Doug
exchange a look. Charlotte takes over the telling of the tale.)* Meine
Tante Luise was working on an estate in East Prussia, and she raised
horses. On a large farm. And since she was fifteen year old, she
never wore ladies' clothes.
    No.
    Only boots. And jodphurs. The clothes of a Land Inspector,
and not a fine lady. *(She gives a long, knowing look to punctuate that
thought. Then she continues.)* And so I was coming in August in
1943 to East Prussia and I found in her closet clothes. Girl's
clothes. And ... *(She whispers with an almost erotic intensity:)* ... I
... put ... them ... on. *(Charlotte steps before an imaginary mirror.
She gazes into as if she were looking at herself — truly examining herself — for the first time. And she's delighted by her image in the glass.
She turns, raising the skirt like some exotic fan. Suddenly, she's strick-
en by a look of terror. She sees another reflection, looming behind her.)*
And my aunt was coming into the room, and I was standing there,
and she looked at us in the mirror, and then she said: *(Charlotte
becomes Tante Luise, with a stirring alto voice:)*
TANTE LUISE.  *"Weisst du, mit uns beiden hat die Natur sich einen
Scherz erlaubt. Du hättest ein Madchen werden müssen und ich ein
Mann!" (She repeats the phrase — eloquently — in English:)* Did you
know that nature has dared to play a joke on us? You should've
been born a girl, and I should've been a man! *(Tante Luise morphs
back into Charlotte:)*
CHARLOTTE.  And there was — on the bookshelf — a book. And
meine Tante took this book down and handed it to me. The binding,
it was blue. And I opened it. And on its *Titelbild* — "frontispiece" —
*"Die Transvestiten, by Magnus Hirschfeld." Und ich spürte eine
Gänsehaut ... über meinen Rücken kriechen.* I felt a shiver down my
spine. And meine Tante Luise said "read." *(Charlotte begins to read:)*
In each person, there is a delicate balance of male and female sub-
stances. Just as we can't find two matching leaves from the same tree,
it is scientifically impossible to find two human beings whose male
and female characteristics match in kind and number. *(She passes the
book to Doug. To Doug:)* Read. *(Now he reads from the text:)*
DOUG.  And so we must treat sexual intermediaries — those indi-

viduals who defy the ready classification of "man" or "woman" —
as a common ... utterly natural ... phenomenon? *(He looks to
Charlotte for approval; she nods and says:)*
CHARLOTTE. Yes. And meine Tante said:
TANTE LUISE. This book is not just any book. This book, it will
be your Bible.
CHARLOTTE. *(To Doug, lightheartedly.) Möchten Sie ein paar
Spritzkuchen? (Doug ducks aside, his invisible tape recorder primed,
and makes a few private observations.)*

## SUPERTITLE: THE GIVE-AWAY

DOUG. Charlotte's just slipped into the kitchen, to bring us some
*Kaffee und Kuchen.* I brought a camera, but I'm too shy to ask her to
pose ... I'm afraid she'll think I've only come to gawk. So I wanted
to record a quick ... visual ... an impression.
    She's about five eight, maybe a hundred and seventy pounds.
Sixty-five years old. Doesn't look like drag queen *at all.* No make-
up. I asked her about that; she says she "doesn't need it." She's got
piercing eyes — really smart eyes — and a sly, little crooked smile.
She still wears her own hair, white, goose-feather white, cut in —
I guess you'd call it a "page-boy." She's got on a black peasant dress,
a string of pearls, and heavy, black shoes. Orthopedic shoes.
    She doesn't have breasts, not really, but just enough paunch to
sort of enhance the impression.
    But her hands are big, and thick. The hands of a woodworker.
Of a craftsman. Definitely a man's hands. *(Doug raises his own
hands as if they belonged to Charlotte. As he does so, he transforms back
into her. Charlotte puts another Edison Amberol on the phonograph,
and the room fills with the sound of nostalgia.)*

## SUPERTITLE: ARE YOU A BOY OR A GIRL?

CHARLOTTE. And the last days of the World War were the most
dangerous time for me because I refused to carry a weapon or to
wear a uniform. Instead, I had my hair long and blonde and my
mother's coat, and the shoes of a girl. And so I was — in Germany,

we say *"Freiwild."* Like the Jews, we were wild game.

Berlin was destroyed. I was walking about — the houses were all broken — and the street was full of rubble. Yes. And I would turn a street, and there was coming Russian airplanes with the Splatter Bombs — so close, you could see the pilot with the helmet and the goggles. And this was very dangerous, because — wherever you were standing — the splatter bombs exploded into the earth. Pieces went everywhere. There was no escape.

And there was — on the corner — standing an air raid shelter. And so I went inside. And I was sitting there maybe half an hour.

And I could hear the bombs, and the old building was shaking. And suddenly the door opened, and in came four SS Officers. Infantry police. *Die Kettenhunde.*

And they were looking for boys and men and old men which were hiding, without weapons. And so they dragged me up, to the police station. And I had to stand outside against the wall.

The SS Men were standing four, maybe five meters away. *(She becomes the SS Officer, and plays out the scene in real time.)*

SS OFFICER. *(Doctrinaire.)* All deserters shall be shot.

CHARLOTTE. And they wanted to shoot me. I looked down; I didn't want to see them shoot. I thought, "I'll wait until I feel it." But when I looked to the ground. I saw the boots of a Commander. *(Her gaze rises as she sizes up the Commander with both awe and dread.)* And he looked at me.

SS COMMANDER. Are you a boy or a girl?

CHARLOTTE. And I thought, "If they shoot me, what's the difference between a boy and a girl, because dead is dead!" *(She becomes a child and answers:)*

YOUNG LOTHAR. I am a boy.

SS COMMANDER. How old are you then?

YOUNG LOTHAR. Sixteen.

CHARLOTTE. And he turned around to face the Execution Squad Commander.

SS COMMANDER. *(With some measure of self-contempt.)* We are not so far gone that we have to shoot school children.

CHARLOTTE. And this was my salvation. *(Charlotte lifts the needle off the wax roll, and becomes Doug.)*

## SUPERTITLE: LISTENING

DOUG.  My dear Charlotte,
   Enclosed please find two antique cylinders. Your favorite: John Philip Sousa. *El Capitan* and *Semper Fidelis*. They're Blue Amberols, so you should be able to play them on your Edison Standard.
   I — meanwhile — am listening to our interview tapes every chance I get. On the treadmill. In the car. I've also started reading the works of Magnus Hirschfeld, and studying German history since the time of Wilhelm II. Still, all I can think about is the story of your life. *(Then with feeling:)* You are teaching me a history I never knew I had. Thank you. *(A pause.)* Tape Seven. January 26, 1993.
CHARLOTTE.  *Heute habe ich einen Spitznamen fur dich.*
DOUG.  A nickname? For me?
CHARLOTTE.  "Thomas Alva Edison." *(Charlotte smiles inscrutably, then sits.)* You have a talking machine, too, yes? Only his was made of tinfoil with a tiny stylus, and yours … yours is a … *(She leans in to read the inscription on Doug's tape recorder:)* … "Sony Microcasette Recorder with voice-activation and automatic playback." Hmmm.
DOUG.  *(Grinning.)* Charlotte's boyhood. Continued from previous tape. *(Charlotte begins to speak.)*

## SUPERTITLE: VATERLAND

CHARLOTTE.  When I was a baby and then a little child —
DOUG.  Can I interrupt you for a moment, and play that back? I'm not sure — the batteries —
CHARLOTTE.  Hmm. Yes, of course. *(Doug futzes with the tape recorder.)*
TAPE RECORDING.  *(The voice of Charlotte.)* "When I was a baby and then a little child — "
DOUG.  We're good. Go ahead.
CHARLOTTE.  My father was a Nazi. *(Doug reacts.)* And he was brutal. And he was for militarism. And the years of marriage for my mother was a moratorium. My mother, she wanted to *sich scheiden ʼssen.* Get a divorce. And my aunt said one day to me:

18

TANTE LUISE. If your father beats your mother once more, she could die.

CHARLOTTE. And it was luck for us that in 1943 in Berlin the government decreed the evacuation of mothers with children, because of the air raids. And so my mother took the children to East Prussia, to the house of my aunt. And at that time we became good friends. Because my aunt was a lesbian and I was the same.

And one day, I was cleaning the furniture, and I looked through the window and it was snowing, and there was coming in the snow a man with a hat and a bag and I became horribly scared because I realized this was my father.

And my aunt and my father had a very heart discussion. And my aunt said:

TANTE LUISE. Your wife really wants a divorce from you.

CHARLOTTE. And suddenly my father pulled out a revolver, and pointed it at my aunt. And he said:

HERR BERFELDE. One more word and I'll shoot you.

CHARLOTTE. But my aunt took her revolver from the desk and said:

TANTE LUISE. I'll count to three, and then you better be out the door! Otherwise, I'll shoot.

CHARLOTTE. And she said:

TANTE LUISE. ... three!

CHARLOTTE. *Und die Kugel durchschlug das Holz und blieb in der gegenüberliegenden Tür stecken* — the bullet went through one door and into the next, where it lodged, and my father returned to Berlin. And then I asked my aunt, and she said:

TANTE LUISE. Yes, of course. It's a shame I didn't kill him.

CHARLOTTE. Then — on the twenty-sixth of January 1945 — my mother got a letter saying the government was taking over our house for Berliners who had lost their homes in the bombing. And so I went with the train to Berlin because I had to rearrange the furniture. To make room for the refugees. *(Charlotte seats herself at the table of antique models; it now suggests the house of her childhood, rendered in miniature. The scene seems to play out — doll-sized — in front of her.)* And so I was coming into our house, and my father was living here, of course. And one evening maybe it was the second or third day — no, I think it was a week — it was in the first week of February 1945 — and one evening my father said to me:

HERR BERFELDE. This is the hour I ask you. Are you for me or your mother? Do you stand beside her or me?

19

CHARLOTTE. I was fifteen years old. And I asked him, "Aren't you ashamed of the way you've treated my mother?" And he said:

HERR BERFELDE. I'll shoot you down like a dog, and then I'll go to East Prussia and shoot your mother and your sister and your brother.

CHARLOTTE. And I thought of the words of my aunt. And I know that my father would do this.

He locked me in the bedroom by turning the key. Because it was war, I could hear the Allied Bombs, coming in the night. And then under the bed I saw such a large wooden utensil used to mixing cake — *wie sagt man* — a rolling pin. And I thought, I can take this as a weapon.

I wanted to sneak out the door, but it was tightly locked. But even then, I had in my pocket ... keys. So I very carefully opened the door, and I was going in the next room.

It was very dark, except for a little moonlight which was shining. And I saw my father. He was lying on the sofa in the dining room, and his gun lay on the chair next to him. And I saw the chair. I saw the pistol. And in that moment, the clock — we had a Westminster clock — and the clock was chiming, and I saw my father's hand; he was reaching for his weapon. And in this moment I began beating him. *(She says with sudden ferocity:) Eins! Zwei! Drei! Vier! Fünf! (A pause. She dissociates for a moment, becoming oddly contemplative.)* Hmm. Yes.

And the next day, the Criminal Police came. And they asked me for the motive. And I told them. And when I was arrested, they brought me before the Youth Justice. And I was sentenced to the Youth Prison in Tegel. Four years detention. And when they took me to the jail, my mother was there. And we looked at each other in the eyes, and we knew that we were finally free from the monster. *(Charlotte bolts up from the table and becomes Doug, frantically scribing a letter:)*


## SUPERTITLE: AUF DEUTSCH


DOUG. Oh, John!

I'm in way over my head. To kill: *"töten, tötete, hat getötet."* *Christ, this language doesn't make any sense.*

I'm still winding my way through *Die Transvestiten*. Sigh. In some sentences, I can barely discern the verb. And the vocabulary I'm learning is … well … so *specific*. Yesterday in German class, I made an ass out of myself. The teacher told us to make "small talk." I froze; couldn't remember a single phrase. So I blurted out a few new words I'd translated the night before.

"*Hi, ich bin Doug, und ich trage schwarze Spitzenunterwäsche.*"

"Hi, my name's Doug and I'm wearing black lace panties!"

The whole class just stared at me. Except for this one guy named Morris, who offered to take me shopping. Maybe I should try reading something else?

Love,

Doug. *(Once again, Doug readies an interview tape for Charlotte.)*

## SUPERTITLE: DURCH DIE LUFT

DOUG. Tape Nine. March 5, 1993. *(Doug practices a few, innocuous lines of German.)* "*Guten Abend,* Charlotte. *Und wie geht es* Dir *heute? Wie geht es* Ihnen *heute?*" *(He appears at Charlotte's door. He greets Charlotte in her native tongue.)* Guten abend, Charlotte.

CHARLOTTE. *Guten abend.*

DOUG. *Ich habe Deutsch gelernt, um Dein phantastisches Leben besser zu verstehen.*

CHARLOTTE. Excuse me?

DOUG. *Jetzt sollen wir Deutsch sprechen, ja?*

CHARLOTTE. You are learning to speak German?

DOUG. *Ein bischen, ja. Ich habe mit Berlitz studiert.*

CHARLOTTE. You speak German. Me, English. I wear your clothes, and you wear mine.

DOUG. *Als das Ende des Kriegs kam, waren Sie noch im Gefängnis?*

CHARLOTTE. The Youth Penitentiary at Tegel? *Nein.* A miracle allowed me to escape, yes? I was serving my sentence, sitting on a cot, brushing my hair with an old ivory comb from meine Tante. And I heard a guard cry in the hallway:

PRISON GUARD. The Russians! They're flying over our roof!

CHARLOTTE. And it was true! Soon, the bombs began to fall! The walls, they toppled down like sand-castles in the tide. And the Guard cried "Run!" And so I picked up my blanket and my alarm clock, and I ran. I ran. I ran. Through the iron gates. Past the r of the old Jewish synagogue. And I saw on the street the large Russian tanks. And behind the tanks were coming horses with painted wagons. The Allies were coming to Berlin. And then there came a coach with the officers! Decorated. Yes, yes. Russian soldiers and they were giving loaves of bread to the people!

And it was spring! And the birds were singing in the trees! And it was an awful war.

## SUPERTITLE: EINE SPENDE

*A telephone rings; short, European tones. It rings again. And again.*

ANSWERING MACHINE. *(The voice of John.)* "*Sie haben die Wohnung von John Marks erreicht. Bitte hinterlassen Sie eine Nachricht nach dem Pfeifton.*"
DOUG. Are you there? Hello? Anybody home? *(A protracted beep.)* … Christ, pick up, pick up, pick up … *(John picks up.)*
JOHN. *(Groggy.)* Huh?
DOUG. John?
JOHN. Doug?
DOUG. Listen, I've run out of grant money, so I'm canceling my May trip. But all is not lost — I've decided to sell my car —
JOHN. — you ever heard of Time Zones? — it's four fucking A.M. —
DOUG. — It's an '86 Honda Civic, and I think I can get about three thousand dollars for it — That should finance at least a month overseas, maybe more —
JOHN. Whoa, whoa, whoa. You're gonna *sell your car?* Don't you think you're going a little loopy?
DOUG. *(A burst of frustration.)* John…! *(Impassioned:)* Don't you see? She doesn't run a museum, she is one! The rarest artifact she has isn't a grandfather clock or a Beidermeier tall-boy. It's her. *(In slow, measured tones.)* So please. If I come in June, can I still crash on your floor? *(A pause, and then Doug speaks into his recorder, triumphant:)* Tape Fifteen. *June 20, 1993.* *(Charlotte smiles enigmatically, and gestures for Doug to follow.)*
CHARLOTTE. Careful; you must watch the stairs. Today, you

follow me at your own risk. I show you *das Geheimnis* — the secret — of *meinem Gründerzeit Museum.* *(Doug obliges.)*

DOUG. *(Into tape.)* Charlotte's disappearing down a series of steps; I guess I'm supposed to go down after her. Christ, it's steep. Now we're in the basement, I think, of the house. It's dark. She's lighting a gas lamp. *(Doug looks about the room in wonder.)* Holy shit. It's huge. Old-fashioned, rough-hewn tables on wrought-iron stands. Cane-back chairs. There's an enormous bar, made of oak, stocked high with glasses, liquors, and — it's porcelain — I can't quite tell — but it might be an ancient beer pump.

## SUPERTITLE: MULACK RITZE

CHARLOTTE. Welcome to *die Mulack-Ritze.* An old tavern from the Yesterday.

DOUG. The walls are mottled and old. Signs, everywhere. There's one, written in thin script on yellowed paper:

CHARLOTTE. "Prostitution is strictly forbidden! At least, according to the police."

DOUG. On a placard in bold type:

CHARLOTTE. *"Tanzen ist Verboten."* Dancing is forbidden. But we had this old phonograph — *mit einem Blumentrichter* — and we would dance in the back, *ja?*

A long time ago, this old bar was sitting in the barn district of Berlin on *Mulack Straße* Number Fifteen. From the time of the Emperor Wilhelm II, it was a restaurant for gays and lesbians. The owners wanted homosexuals because they didn't get drunk, they didn't fight, and they always had money for to pay for the bill.

At this very table *haben* Bertolt Brecht, Marlene Dietrich, the sexologist Magnus Hirschfeld *und* the actress Henny Porten *alle gesessen, ja?* This table, he is over one hundred years old. If I could I would take an old gramphone needle and run it along the surface of wood. To hear the music of the voices. All that was said.

Minna Mahlich, she was the barmaid, *ja?* And in 1963, she came to me and she said:

MINNA MAHLICH. The *Kommunisten,* they want to close us down. *Unsere Geschichte ist dekadent, ja?* Our history is decadent We have only one day. And then, "the bull-dozers."

CHARLOTTE. And I thought, "That is not good."

23

So I bought this furniture — I paid a little bit of money — and I bought it for this museum here. Everything — every glass — is original, *ja?* I took it all with me here for safety and I hid it in *meinem Keller.* And the next day, the Russians came, and the old bar on *Mulack Straße,* they broke it down.

And then came the wall. And for us here in Eastern Berlin, it was finished, gay life. The bars, closed. Personal advertisements in the newspaper, canceled. No place to meet but the tramway stations and the public toilets. We were not supposed to exist. *Persona non grata.*

So I thought to give homosexual women and men community in this house. Yes. It was a museum for all people, but I thought, "Why not for homosexuals?"

So we met here — in *die Mulack-Ritze* — on the Sunday afternoons. And sometimes in front of the crowd Minna would run a finger along the bar, and when it came up black with dust, she'd cry:
MINNA MAHLICH.  Charlotte, you pig! You haven't cleaned!
CHARLOTTE.  And I'd tell the visitors, this is a historic moment! This is Minna Mahlich, the last owner of the *Mulack-Ritze.* And the people would all clap and laugh.

And there was over the bar, an attic. When a boy or girl met a man, and wanted to go upstairs, they could. Two men, two girls, a boy and a girl — it didn't matter. And they'd go into this room. A divan, a sofa, a chaise lounge, a bed. A screen separated each space. Every piece of furniture was always in use. A pair in every free seat!

And anyone with an interest in sadomasochism — whether it was two or four or six — could have the room to themselves for a few hours. Whips and things to beat on the behind.

And the Stasi — the Communist secret police, the most feared government spies of all the world — was coming, and they were looking in the windows, and they were saying, "What's this?" So what could I do? I painted all the windows black. *(Doug speaks reverently — in hushed tones — into his own recorder:)*
DOUG.  When the wall falls — Charlotte tells me — she had the only surviving Weimar Cabaret in all of Eastern Germany. Hidden in the basement of her house in Mahlsdorf. Which she ran — under the watchful eye of the Stasi — for almost thirty years. *(Suddenly, a blast of pompous music. The Minister of Cultural Affairs approaches the podium to make a speech:)*

# SUPERTITLE: BUNDESVERDIENSTKREUZ

CULTURAL MINISTER. On behalf of the Cultural Minstry of the *Bundesrepublik Deutschland*, it gives me great joy and honor, in recognition of your astonishing efforts at conservation — your steadfast preservation of a noted period in German industrial design –– *(Charlotte intercedes, to ensure he says it correctly:)*
CHARLOTTE. — *die Gründerzeit* —
CULTURAL MINISTER. *(Utterly charmed by Charlotte.)* — *die Gründerzeit* — and your timely rescue of the *Mulack-Ritze,* to offer you membership in the high order of the *Bundesrepublik Deutschland* and deliver unto you the medal of honor — a cross upon a ribbon. *(The music amps, followed by thunderous applause and cheers. Charlotte curtsies. The sound fades.)*
CHARLOTTE. The day I received the medal was for me recognition of my work, and I thought –– *wie soll ich sagen* — I thought it's good because other people see that a transvestite can work. A transvestite becomes such a medal! If other people — heterosexual people –– they look at the television, and they read the newspapers and they say, "Ah! He or she is able to work, *ja.*"
JOHN. They presented the award on national German television. Aw, Doug, I wish you could've been there. Picture it. An elderly man, in a skirt and a string of pearls. Nobody laughed. No cat-calls. And — at the end of the ceremony — the Cultural Minister himself even leaned down to kiss her hand.

# SUPERTITLE: BERLIN FROM BEHIND

DOUG. *(To Charlotte.)* Charlotte, what was it like? To visit the West after the wall came down? *(A sudden blast of music; it's cheesy German disco, a song like "Super Paradise."\* Charlotte smoothes the creases in her skirt and plucks a small guidebook called* Berlin von Hinten *from the table. A few well-placed steps across the stage, and she's crossed the border into Western Berlin. She reaches a particular address, and admires the façade of an imagined building. She consul her guidebook, and reads aloud:)*

\* See Special Note on Songs and Recordings on copyright page.

CHARLOTTE. "Café Anal. The crowd is gay and lesbian, leftist punks and muesli freaks. Sunday night is two-for-one beer blast. Other events include gay slide shows about South America, karaoke, and drag-queen bingo!" *(Charlotte raises an eyebrow, then moves on, dancing ever so slightly to the throbbing beat.)* "Buddy's Bar. The dignified ambience of black leather is enhanced with hot music and stimulating porn-videos and a young boy can usually be persuaded to give a little show." *(Charlotte folds down the corner of the page; this pub is definitely worth remembering. A final stop on her whirlwind tour:)* "Prinz Eisenherz Buchladen. This gay bookstore stocks everything ever written by homophiles, nancies, pansies, sissies, trannies, sodomites, Sapphists, fruitcakes, homos, faggots, lezzies, dykes, queens, queers, gender-benders and friends of Dorothy." *(Charlotte balks. Muttering to herself:)* I don't know what that means ... *(The music stops. Doug asks — in measured tones:)*
DOUG. Now Charlotte, I heard in the seventies the Stasi came to you, and offered to treat you very well if you would give the names and addresses of the people who frequented your museum. I heard they actually promised you a car. Is that right?

## SUPERTITLE: I, LOTHAR BERFELDE

*Charlotte's demeanor changes; she speaks cautiously.*

CHARLOTTE. Yes. And one day, they came, and one of the two men said to me:
STASI OFFICIAL. You have to sit down. Take a paper and a pencil, and I will dictate to you the following ...
CHARLOTTE. *(Suspiciously.)* And I thought, "What's that?"
DOUG. *(With certainty.)* So you didn't do it?
CHARLOTTE. *(Indignant:)* He wanted me to write exactly what he said!
DOUG. *(With apprehension.)* And what was the text you were expected to write? *(Charlotte picks up a slip of paper from the table; she reads haltingly:)*
CHARLOTTE. "I, Lothar Berfelde, commit myself willingly and ~ely to working together with the Ministry for State Security. I ⌐ report all information which may have the character of an

26

action inimical to the state." *(She pauses. It's difficult to continue, but she manages:)* "I will be known by the code name Park. I pledge to keep this secret even from my nearest friends and relatives." *(Another pause; she thinks of her mother. Of her siblings. Then — staunchly — to Doug, the end of the pledge.)* "I have been informed that if I break this oath, I will be prosecuted according to the laws of the GDR."

DOUG. *(Hoping against hope.)* And you had to sign it?

CHARLOTTE. *(Quietly, definitively:)* I signed it. *(Tension fills the room.)* And I said to myself, "I'll still do whatever I want." *Ich mache doch was ich will.*

DOUG. And then they left.

CHARLOTTE. *Ja, ja. (Another pause. Charlotte turns cagey:) Meine* Tante Luise always said, "Be as smart as the snakes; it's in the Bible." She said, "Never forget that you are living in the lion's den. Sometimes, you must howl with the wolves." *(John bounds out of Charlotte's chair.)*


## SUPERTITLE: BATED BREATH


JOHN. Doug. Listen up. *(Beat.)* The German press got its hands on Charlotte's Stasi file. She was an informant, all right. For four years, in the mid-seventies. It says she was "willing." Even "enthusiastic." And that museum of hers? It was a drop-off point for secret packages and documents of interest to the Stasi. Charlotte reported on illegal antique dealings. It even says she was responsible for an arrest. And not just anyone. A fellow collector. A friend.

The tabloids are having a field day. I've enclosed a few clippings. *(Doug sifts through them, finding each new headline more incredible than the last.)*

DOUG. "Charlotte von Mahlsdorf, Sexual Outlaw and Soviet Spy?" *(Beat.)* "Mata Hari was Man; the Real Story of Berlin's Most Notorious Transvestite." *(Beat.)* "Comrade Charlotte: Is the Disguise She's Wearing More Than Just a Dress?" *(Beat.)* John? I'll get back to Berlin just as soon as I can. *(Once again — from the phonograph — the mesmerizing lilt of a German waltz. Charlotte dances, a quiet little reverie, all to herself.)*

CHARLOTTE.   Even when I was a little child, no one wanted phonographs. Everyone said to me, "It's so old fashioned!" They all wanted radios. But what did I want with a radio? To hear Hitler babble? No thank you! That is the reason that even today I don't have a radio or a television.

For me, gramophones, polyphons, pianolas — I must truly say — these machines gave me so much pleasure in my childhood. If I hadn't had them, I'm not sure I would've survived. Things were so ghastly with my father — everything my mother and I went through.

But the music would pour through the horn and make things better. *(And it carries her away, into some distant corner of her own mind.)*

## End of Act One

# ACT TWO

*In the darkness, the rollicking sound of an old pianola. Unexpectedly, it ends with the loud slam of a prison door. Lights rise on Alfred Kirschner, lying on the floor of his prison cell, striated by light. He looks a bit like a cockroach that's been flipped on its back, helplessly. Alfred's prison uniform hangs on his thin bones like sails on a mast. His glasses are thick, distorting his eyes. His cap is woolen and patched. He has a caustic wit. Slowly, he rises to a sitting position and addresses Charlotte as if she were the audience.*

## SUPERTITLE: A LETTER FROM PRISON

ALFRED. The seventeenth of April, 1972.
   Dear Charlotte,
   I was dining at lunch — a scrumptious vegetable stew with mashed potatoes — *(He bellows down the prison corridor to some unseen cook:)* — truly exquisite — *(Then he turns back to Charlotte and resumes.)* — when your note arrived. Today's the day I put aside to answer letters, and I thought, "Well if I don't get any mail today, I'll just stop writing altogether. Then I'll die, lost and forgotten by the world." So it came in the nick of time. You urged me, "Don't give up! You're not forgotten! You never had hordes of friends, but so what? You always gave a little joy to people, and that's enough." What sweet sentiments, Charlotte. For your sake, I won't give up, and I'll live patiently for the day I'll be set free.
   At night, I wrap myself in blankets. I still have headaches and dizzy spells, but I don't think it's the fault of prison conditions. I think it's just age. I've gone so blind I can barely read. I just wander from one doctor to the next. They zap you with electricity, record it on paper and — voilà — an electrocardiograph. The dentist here is a real dictator. He plans to pull another one of my teeth. By the time you get this letter, I'll probably be nothing but gums. Alfred sans teeth is not a pretty sight! *(Alfred curls his lips over his gums to appear toothless and grimaces to illustrate his point.)* Please give your family my wa

29

regards. Tell them I'm still the same old Alfred — *(To a prison guard somewhere in the darkness:)* — *and I won't be beaten down! (Again, back to Charlotte:)* When I'm released, I know exactly what I'll do. I'll play my favorite old waltz on the piano. Strauss, probably. Then I'll put *"Frühlingskinder"* on the polyphon, and play that, too.

With a calliopic and symphonic farewell —

Your Alfred. *(Alfred removes his glasses and becomes Doug. Doug stares at the glasses, considering them a moment.)*


## SUPERTITLE: ERASURE


DOUG.  Charlotte,

I'm afraid — for me — your Stasi file is an exercise in frustration. *(Doug rests the glasses upside down on a nearby sideboard. As he speaks, he pulls off Alfred's beret. Beneath it, Charlotte's black kerchief.)* I've noticed repeated references to a fellow antique collector; sometimes, they use the word *Kunsthandler.* Other times, *Sammler.* But whenever his actual name appears, it's been blacked out. I turn the pages over, I hold them up to the light, and still I can't make it out. *(Doug unbuttons Alfred's shirt to reveal Charlotte's blouse and pearls. He lowers Alfred's trousers, and — under them — Charlotte's pleated black skirt.)* "Today, the informant Park had tea with BLANK. Park received a birthday card from BLANK. At 2:30 p.m. in the afternoon, Park telephoned BLANK." *(Doug now stands in Charlotte's signature garb. He puts Alfred's clothes in the sideboard.)* I suspect BLANK was important to you. Otherwise, why would he merit inclusion in your file?

Please. Shed light, if you can. *(Delicately, Charlotte uprights Alfred's old glasses; he seems to stare out at her from a shelf on the sideboard. She considers him a moment, fondly.)*


## SUPERTITLE: MYTHOLOGY


CHARLOTTE.  I still have his birth certificate. Alfred Kirschner, born on the first of September, 1911.

We became friends because it was a rainy day. I was walking through the streets of Berlin, and I saw an antiquity shop. I had no money to buy old things, I only wanted to stay dry. As I strolled through the stock, I glanced around the corner, and I saw Alfred. He was looking at a polyphon. *(She turns to Alfred, adopting both roles:)* Do you own such a machine?

ALFRED. Of course. I'm a collector. I've been a collector since my childhood.

CHARLOTTE. I am a collector since my childhood, too!

ALFRED. Back at my house ... just two or three blocks from here ... I have about 15,000 records.

CHARLOTTE. *(Flirtatiously.)* Touché! I only have 12,000.

ALFRED. And where do you live?

CHARLOTTE. *(Flouncing her skirts, ever-so-slightly.)* In Mahlsdorf. Across from the pig farm. Near the paper factory. *(She turns to us:)* With that, Alfred bought a few music boxes.

ALFRED. The weather is so awful today; why not pay me a visit in *Mulack Straße?* Mahlsdorf's a long way in this maelstrom.

CHARLOTTE. *(With recognition and delight.)* Mulack Straße? That's where you live?

ALFRED. What about it?

CHARLOTTE. Remember the old pub, the *Mulack-Ritze?* Now it's in my museum!

ALFRED. *(With a hint of seduction.)* I've heard of your museum, and of you — but now I'm meeting you in the flesh ...

CHARLOTTE. And so off we went to his apartment. He made some *Kaffee mit schlag und Kuchen.* And we played a large polyphon. And it wasn't long before he said:

ALFRED. Look in my private room.

CHARLOTTE. And I did. And there were records everywhere. Whole shelves. He had Caruso records. Comedians, dance orchestras, jazz, opera. Polyphons, gramophones, phonographs, juke boxes, symphonions, pianolas, spieldosen, orchestrions, echophones, calliopes, Victrolas, Edison standards, amberols, paperolls, hurdy-gurdies, organettes. Clocks, too. Wall clocks, mantel clocks, grandfather clocks, regulators by Lenzkirch and Gustav Becker, cuckoo clocks, alarm clocks, chronometers and pocket watches. A breastplate from the Middle Ages. Of course, everybody knew that Alfred was homosexual. Later, I'd visit his house. Sometimes homosexual men were standing before his door, like prostitutes. *(A young man idles at Alfred's stoop, insolently smoking a rolled cigarette.)*

YOUNG HOMOSEXUAL MAN. You can't ring Alfred now. He has one man or two men with him. Just wait till he's ready, whe he's done with his sexuality.

CHARLOTTE. No! I just came to swap gramophone records.

YOUNG HOMOSEXUAL MAN. Oh, you're a transvestite!

CHARLOTTE. And how they cackled until Alfred opened the door to let me in. *(Charlotte steps into a focused pool of light, adopting the role of narrator in the upcoming tale.)* One day, Alfred bought a clock from a local antique dealer. He was headed home down *Mulack Straße,* and he noticed that a motor car was following him. And in this motor car there were two army soldiers from the American base. One of the soldiers rolled down the car window: *(The American Soldier has a decidedly Midwestern accent.)*

AMERICAN SOLDIER. Hey, can we buy that clock off you?

ALFRED. Not this one; it's mine.

AMERICAN SOLDIER. My mom said I couldn't come home without a clock. One of those black forest jobs. Man, that'd look sweet back in Terre Haute.

ALFRED. I do have other clocks I'm willing to sell.

AMERICAN SOLDIER. Oh yeah?

CHARLOTTE. And the soldiers trooped into *Mulack Straße,* into his apartment, where he had nine or ten regulators for sale.

ALFRED. *(To the two soldiers.)* Take your pick.

AMERICAN SOLDIER. Beautiful. We'll take two.

CHARLOTTE. At that time — in the seventies — people thought gaudy old standing clocks were just old-fashioned junk. Kitsch. In Berlin, you could pick up a grandfather clock for, maybe, fifty marks. Very cheap!

AMERICAN SOLDIER. Shit, Sergeant Matheson paid twice that on the Ku' damm. *(Charlotte does a double-take at the soldier, a bit taken aback at his interruption. He cowers apologetically. She continues with her tale.)*

CHARLOTTE. Anyway. Not long after that, Alfred came to me with a proposition.

ALFRED. *(The wheeler-dealer.)* People are always giving you clocks as gifts. Half the time, you don't want them. They're early twentieth century, and that's too modern for your museum —

CHARLOTTE. Alfred … what are you suggesting …

ALFRED. I've got a friend named Edward. He's got an automobile. We can drive to Pankow, to the woods near Weissensee — with the clocks in tow —

CHARLOTTE. *(Intrigued in spite of herself.)* Yes?

ALFRED. We'll sell a bundle, right out of the back of the car.

CHARLOTTE. Sure enough, the American soldiers came, and they looked into the back of Edward's car.

AMERICAN SOLDIER. — these are damn nice —

ALFRED. Why not buy them all, as souvenirs? To send back home. How many have I got here? Nine, ten, eleven …

AMERICAN SOLDIER. Hell, our car isn't big enough. *(The glorious dawning of an idea.)* We'll come next week with a little bus.

CHARLOTTE. So we met them again the following week.

AMERICAN SOLDIER. Hey. We're back. *(Sotto voce, to his buddy:)* See, I told you — *one of these dudes wears a dress* —

CHARLOTTE. Into the bus they put one, two, three, four clocks. And they prepared to drive across the border, back into Western Berlin.

CUSTOMS OFFICIAL. *Halten Sie, bitte.*

AMERICAN SOLDIER. They can't stop us … we're Americans, man.

CUSTOMS OFFICIAL. *Wir müssen diesen Autobus inspizieren.*

AMERICAN SOLDIER. *(To the Customs Official.)* Sure, no prob. *(To his fellow Soldier.)* Hey, Dave. It's friggin' Customs. They want to — like — case our bus … You crazy? You tell 'em "no," I'm not telling 'em "no." Just … holy shit … *just get out of the goddamn bus.* Come on, man, it's not worth it. They're fuckin' *cuckoo clocks,* for Chrissakes. *(Charlotte takes over the narrative again.)*

CHARLOTTE. And they detained the soldiers for six, seven hours. And the border agents wrote down the number of their bus. And the Stasi started keeping a list of all our little sales. And the next time the bus came to meet us, they followed it with an automobile of their own. Some months later, Alfred heard a knock on his door.

STASI AGENT. We have reason to believe that you're engaging in illegal sales, with foreign military personnel. We hope — for your sake — we have made a grave error in judgment.

CHARLOTTE. Alfred came back to me. Naturally, I expected him to mend his ways.

ALFRED. *(Incorrigible as ever.)* Lottchen, I've an idea. Why don't we sell the clocks out of your basement instead of the car?

CHARLOTTE. But Alfred —

ALFRED. There's no other place in all of Eastern Berlin quite so secret.

CHARLOTTE. So Alfred brought the clocks around to my place, and we stashed them here. Right here, in this basement corridor there were five, six, seven clocks. Standing in the darkness, like ser tinels, *ja? (The stage is plunged into near-darkness, except for a small light illuminating Charlotte. We hear the ticking of an enormous clock.)* And then at midnight:

ALFRED. *Lottchen!* Open the door! We're in terrible danger.

CHARLOTTE. What now?

ALFRED. They followed us. The Stasi came to my apartment. They tore through my desk, they found Western currency. Tomorrow they're coming to see you —

CHARLOTTE. What can I do, hm? I'll bolt the door.

ALFRED. Save yourself, *Lottchen.* Renounce me.

CHARLOTTE. Don't be ridiculous —

ALFRED. Tell them the clocks are mine —

CHARLOTTE. I could never!

ALFRED. Why should we both go to prison?

CHARLOTTE. I won't say such a thing — I *can't* —

ALFRED. They'll force their way into your house. They'll go traipsing into the basement, into the bar, they'll confiscate your polyphons and your pianolas — they'll take your sideboard and your *vertiko* —

CHARLOTTE. *Quatsch! Du bist zu dramatisch!*

ALFRED. Listen to me! They'll auction off your entire collection, and all to fill their own fat coffers —

CHARLOTTE. *Das ist nicht möglich. Das können sie nicht tun.*

ALFRED. Your museum will be finished. Through. *(The ear-piercing gong of a clock striking midnight. Charlotte stands, framed by the accusatory white glow of Stasi searchlights.)*

CHARLOTTE. So when the Stasi came ... *(She sits. A light shines on her from above, like an interrogation. Her voice cracks and her eyes well with tears.)* "Yes, I have a colleague. Sometimes, he sells clocks to American soldiers. For a little extra money, *ja?* No. I will not write down his name. His address? Certainly not. You must not ask me to take up paper and pen. *That I will not do.*" *(A pause. Charlotte relents.)* "I will say it. I will whisper it only." *(The light softens, and Charlotte resumes the tale.)* And they arrested him. *(The brutal slam of a prison door. Again, the harsh lines of prison light. Alfred pens another note behind bars.)*

ALFRED. My dear Charlotte,

I've been in jail for one week now. When the Stasi discovered that I was a homosexual, they feared I might be labeled a mental defective, and exempt from a trial. But at the institution, Herr Doktor Kreinholz ... may god damn him forever ... he said I was perfectly sane. And so I was thrown to the dogs.

You know they perform a strip search when you're being admitted to prison. Needless to say — with me — they got a big surprise.

CHARLOTTE. *(Reading the letter.) Mein Gott! (She's amused in spite of herself, and imparts the contents to us with a tiny grin.)* They found a cock-ring around Alfred's penis and his nuts. They couldn't get it off, because he had such big private parts. So they sent him to the hospital in the prison to see if they could remove it, but even they couldn't get it off. And finally, a metal specialist came, and he slid a piece of metal between Alfred's ring and his sex organs, and then he sawed it off.

ALFRED. What a sad parting, I told the doctor. I've been wearing that sweet little band of steel for over ten years!

CHARLOTTE. I visited Alfred Kirschner in jail. I had on my red coat with the flared skirt, and my hair was quite long. *(She rises to enter the visitation area, and is stopped by an official.)*

PRISON OFFICIAL. Who are you, and who do you intend to visit today?

CHARLOTTE. I am the wife of Alfred Kirschner, of course. *(He admits her, and she sits before Alfred. She smiles at him fondly, pressing her hand against the glass that separates them, hoping to impart some small measure of hope. Alfred slinks back in his chair, dejected.)*

ALFRED. My cell is too damn cold; my rheumatism. My knees are brittle, like porcelain.

CHARLOTTE. I've brought you some warm clothes.

ALFRED. Have you heard from Edward? Or Minna Mahlich?

CHARLOTTE. They're all afraid. "Guilt by association." They don't want the Stasi investigating their lives, too. *(Charlotte returns to us to finish the story.)* Originally I intended to burn all of Alfred's letters. I was always afraid, if the Stasi searched my house, they would find them and ask, "Why do you keep the correspondence of a criminal?" See — the first letter is crinkled. But I rescued it from the wastepaper basket. Because one day, I felt I'd be able to tell the truth. And today is that time.

Here ... written in his own hand, on the back of *eine Speisekarte* ... a menu from an old restaurant ...

ALFRED. *(As though it were a love letter.)* This is my last will and testament. In the case of my death, I give my entire collection of clocks, records, cylinders and everything else in my possession to Lothar Berfelde, also known as Charlotte von Mahlsdorf. Affectionately, Alfred Kirschner.

CHARLOTTE. While he was incarcerated, his home was broken into, and the Stasi impounded everything that he owned. Just like the Nazis during the deportation of Jewish people, they took all his things. *(She turns in a slow circle, as if gazing upon the ravaged apartment for the first time.)* He was left with only his bed. It was awful.

After his release from jail, I went to the church in Weissensee, and I found Alfred a place in their nursing home. *(Once again, she tries to appear optimistic.)* One day, Alfred, you'll have your own flat again.

ALFRED. *(Bitterly, with contempt.)* No. Never again. I don't want to collect anything anymore.

CHARLOTTE. One night, the telephone rang. It was *eine Krankenschwester.* A nurse on the line.

NURSE. You must come at once. Alfred died tonight.

CHARLOTTE. It's true; he left me everything. All in this small folder. Here's an old bill from the electric company; one he couldn't pay. Here's a picture of Alfred with an Electrola gramophone. Ah! Yes! An old postage stamp, from East Prussia. *(She picks up Alfred's glasses off the sideboard and contemplates them a final time.)* Alfred was more intelligent than I. *(She slides open a drawer and — delicately — places the glasses inside, shutting it gently. A burial.)* Still, that's all he had left; scraps of paper, yes?

## SUPERTITLE: AKTENVERMERK

*John strides forward, commandeering the scene from Charlotte.*

JOHN. Now, Doug, that's one helluva story. That midnight visit? Alfred's heroic offer to take the fall on her behalf? *He begs her to sing like a bird?* It's like some Cold War thriller written by Armistead Maupin. Trouble is, it doesn't scan with the facts in her file. Charlotte was already in deep with the Stasi and had been for at least a year. You think Alfred knew that? Just listen to this: *(A Stasi agent appears in a pool of light. He boasts about Charlotte to his Superior Officer:)*

STASI AGENT. We asked the informant — code name "Park" — if he could gather evidence about the suspect Alfred Kirschner. He assured us that he had Herr Kirschner's absolute trust, and could elicit information without arousing his suspicion.

For the past five months, Park has duly recounted conversations with Herr Kirschner directly to us. He has reported Herr Kirschner's illegal transactions with American soldiers. He has confirmed that Herr Kirschner was routinely offered Western currency in exchange for illicit goods. Customs Officials successfully arrested Alfred Kirschner in the first week of August 1971. We have, of course, granted Park full immunity. He may even merit a promotion. *(The agent disappears. Doug turns to John in protest.)*

DOUG. John! We can't go looking to the Stasi file for facts. Those agents had quotas to fill; supervisors to impress. Reports were doctored all the time! One entry contradicts the next: *(The same Stasi agent reappears. This time, he makes profuse apologies to the same Superior Officer:)*

STASI AGENT. Unfortunately, the informant Park is poorly suited for covert operations. He is too easily distracted by old furniture. His manner of dress is willfully bizarre. His penmanship is so slow, so painstaking — so full of curlicues and frippery — that it's futile to ask for written reports. We are reduced to taking dictation. After forty-eight months of service, mountains of paper-work, and numerous visits to the Gründerzeit Museum — he has yielded nothing useful. And so, we have decided to terminate our association.

## SUPERTITLE: A CONVENIENT LAPSE

DOUG. I went back to Mahlsdorf, file in hand. *(Doug musters his courage to confront Charlotte.)* Charlotte, I know this is difficult. And I know I'm an American, from thousands of miles away … I didn't even really know what the Cold War *was* until it ended … so I've no right to sit in judgement. But about Alfred Kirschner … his arrest … *(Charlotte delicately straightens her pearls.)*

CHARLOTTE. Hmm. Yes. Of course. *(Wafting through the air, the sound of Alfred's old music boxes.)* Here is an old sweater I made for Alfred, when he was in prison. And the buttons — the brass buttons — are from the coat of my Grand Uncle, when he served under the Kaiser himself.

DOUG. But Charlotte, I —

CHARLOTTE. These hands have laid mortar and brick; they have carved walnut. But for Alfred, they learned to knit. *(Beat.)* It is beautiful, yes? *(Charlotte seems lost in her own private, hermetically-sealed world of denial. Suddenly, the driving beat of broadcast news music; a square of light — like a television screen — appears, and the German news anchor steps into it. He double-checks the feed in his ear, then launches into the evening telecast.)*

## SUPERTITLE: THE CROSS

GERMAN NEWS ANCHOR. Should Charlotte von Mahlsdorf be required to relinquish the Medal of Honor? That question is on the minds of Germans everywhere today as news of Charlotte's Stasi involvement continued to dominate headlines. Conservative politician Markus Kaufmann: *(Markus Kaufmann leans forward toward an invisible microphone.)*
MARKUS KAUFMANN. It's terrible. It's a tragedy. If anyone suffered because of her cooperation ... if a human price was paid ... then of course she should be stripped of the medal. It's a civic honor; not a badge of shame.
GERMAN NEWS ANCHOR. Humboldt University student Ulrike Liptsch: *(Ulrike plays with the tips of her long, blonde hair, then tosses it back over her shoulder. Although a serious student of political science, she will one day become a super model.)*
ULRIKE LIPTSCH. My friends and I, we think it's stupid. To take away the medal. We shouldn't even look at Charlotte's Stasi files; we should just burn them. One out of every three citizens was working as an informant. Finger-pointing is pointless; it doesn't unify, it only tears people apart.
GERMAN NEWS ANCHOR. Outspoken former political dissident Josef Rüdiger: *(Josef is a bitter man, with the deep-seated anger that comes from unspeakable suffering.)*
JOSEF RÜDIGER. I spent two years at the Stasi prison in Bautzen. They dislocated my shoulders from my sockets; they forced a catheter up my urinary tract and filled it with alcohol. And still, I uttered no one's name but my own. *(Beat.)* Complicity in this country should always be treated as a criminal act. Hasn't the twentieth century taught us that much?
GERMAN NEWS ANCHOR. The President's office said the prestigious medal had been revoked only once before, when a previous recipient revealed he'd formerly been a member of the SS.

## SUPERTITLE: THE THREE M's

*Charlotte turns to face her Accusers and says with severity:*

CHARLOTTE. *(To Marcus Kaufmann:)* Museum. *(To Ulrike Liptsch:)* Möbel. *(To Josef Rudiger:)* Männer. *(She turns to the audience — all smiles again — to helpfully translate:)* Museum. Furniture. Men. *(Then back to the unseen chorus of critics in a spirited, vehement defense.)* This is the order in which I have lived my life. *(Charlotte again enlists the audience as her confidante and friend, telling them another of her many tales:)* One day, I had an appointment to visit a clock-maker in Kopenick. And on the way, I saw a man. And he said, *"Fräulein, nicht so stolz!* Lady, not so proud!" So I smiled. And I was wearing my leather shorts, and he said to me, "You have such a nice backside. A nice ass for whipping."

And I thought, yes. And he asked me to go inside the public tramway station, to the toilets. But only a few shops away, there was … waiting for me … *eine alte Standuhr* … a standing clock … made of oak, with a perfect mechanism from the last century. And to be late for a clock-maker is *unhöflich.* Too impolite. *(Finally, she turns back to her detractors, emphatic once more:)* For me, there was no choice. *(A blast of Euro-Pop, and sensationalist, hip talk-show host Ziggy Fluß seizes the stage.)*

## SUPERTITLE: CELEBRITY

ZIGGY FLUß. Good evening, Deutschland, and welcome to the Ziggy Fluß show. I'm Ziggy Fluß. Among tonight's special guests … the tiny *Großmutter* with the great big secret … Germany's most controversial transvestite … Berlin's own trannie-granny, Charlotte von Mahlsdorf! *(Applause. Charlotte enters, caught like a doe in headlights. Hesitantly, she approaches her assigned seat, next to Ziggy.)* Good evening, Charlotte!
CHARLOTTE. *Guten Abend.*
ZIGGY FLUß. You're used to the red-hot glare of studio lights, aren't you, Charlotte? You've been on the news, you've done the

talk-show circuit —

CHARLOTTE. Yes.

ZIGGY FLUß. But you still don't own a television, correct?

CHARLOTTE. *Nein.* If I want to look at myself, I look in the mirror, *ja?*

ZIGGY FLUß. *Wunderschön, wunderschön. Eine gute Antwort! (Laughter and applause.)* Tell me, are the rumors true? Have you really decided to move to Sweden?

CHARLOTTE. I was in Stockholm on a tour for my book — *meine Selbstbiographie* — and the people, they have been very kind to me.

ZIGGY FLUß. What about your furniture, eh? All those Gründerzeit goodies. Any plans to open a new museum in Scandinavia?

CHARLOTTE. Yes, of course. An old friend of mine heard I was leaving town. She said to me, "You can't transplant an old tree." I told her, "I am not a tree. I am a flower. And I always carry my flower-pot with me." *(The studio audience loves it; she's so damned enchanting.)*

ZIGGY FLUß. But Berlin's the city that made you a star! How can you leave her behind?

CHARLOTTE. I'm afraid that there is too much violence here.

ZIGGY FLUß. And not just on television, am I right?

CHARLOTTE. A short time after I became the *Bundesverdienstkreuz,* we had a garden party in my museum. Almost *achthundert* people, *ja?* We played Donna Summer on the hi-fi, and everyone was dancing and singing under paper lanterns. And I heard a window smash in my basement. A rock. The Brown plague had come back again. *Kristalnacht* once more.

ZIGGY FLUß. Sure, I read about it. Front page of *Die Morgenpost.* Your museum was vandalized, correct?

CHARLOTTE. The Neo-Nazis knew I was a homosexual. They came over the wall, thirty of them, with flare guns and gas pistols. The gays were all cowards, running inside, but the lesbians stayed to fight. And my friend Sylvia, she was in the cellar, trying to shut the door, and she got a gas pistol in the eye. Her retina was damaged. A young girl from Frankfurt-an-Oder almost died. They cracked open her cranium with an iron stick. *(Ziggy Fluß swallows. His light-weight show has taken a very sudden, very grave turn.)*

ZIGGY FLUß. Holy Christ. *(Charlotte — deep in the story now — rises from her chair, reliving the attack.)*

CHARLOTTE. And I was coming from the cellar with an old pick-axe, and a skinhead met me on the stair. He had a swastika tattooed on his arm, yes?

FIRST NEO-NAZI. Hitler forgot to shove you in an oven in Sachsenhausen!

CHARLOTTE. And I swung and hit the blade in the old banister, splitting it open like a sapling, *ja?* And from behind me, another *laut* voice:

SECOND NEO-NAZI. We should drown you in the Ostsee!

CHARLOTTE. And there was a second, *mit einem Schlagholz;* a club. And I said, "I have met you before! When I was sixteen years old!"

And then *die Polizei* came. And the young men scattered. Like *die Asche,* after a fire. No one was arrested. No one went to jail. *(A pause. Charlotte takes her seat again. Even the pathologically upbeat Ziggy is momentarily wiped out by the raw power of her story.)*

ZIGGY FLUß. *(Below his breath.)* Wow. *Autsch! Die Brutalität. Solche Brutalität.*

CHARLOTTE. My old Victrola, it was smashed. Broken bottles. Electric wires, on the ground.

ZIGGY FLUß. Young people today. It's bad, isn't it? They're hurting, they're disillusioned. They've been promised so much, especially in the East. Reunification. Now they feel they've been had —

CHARLOTTE. It's no excuse —

ZIGGY FLUß. *(Chastened.)* — no; you can't make excuses, can you? —

CHARLOTTE. *Nein. Niemals.*

In Solingen, Turkish women getting burned out of their homes. Asylum-seekers from Yugoslavia being beaten on the streets. Anti-Semitism has come back. So has homophobia. Every day, new threats.

ZIGGY FLUß. Keep talking, Charlotte, and I'll move, too! Ibiza, or maybe Mykonos, right? *(A quick spasm of laughter from the studio; Ziggy silences them with a look. He has a hard-hitting question to ask now.)* Now, Charlotte … you know Ziggy has to ask … your flight from Berlin happens to coincide with recent, widely published news reports about your Stasi involvement. Some of your critics suggest you'd rather skip town than face the prospect of a tarnished reputation here at home …

CHARLOTTE. Hmm. Yes. Of course. *(Charlotte smiles sweetly and answers in careful, deliberate tones.)* In Mahlsdorf, my museum had twenty-three rooms. In Porla-Brunn, I will have only eight

But that is good for a woman my age, yes? Not so much furniture to dust. *(She looks searchingly to the audience for the same warm smiles — the same compassion — her wonderful anecdotes always engender. It's hard to tell ... has she won them over yet again? Or is she met by stony silence? Quietly, compassionately — almost apologetically — Ziggy places a hand on her knee.)*
ZIGGY FLUß. *Fantastisch,* Charlotte, *wirklich fantastisch.* You'll come back and visit us again, won't you?
CHARLOTTE. *Danke schön.*
ZIGGY FLUß. We'll be back after a short break with American singing sensation David Hasselhoff —

## SUPERTITLE: EDITORIALS: A PHANTASMAGORIA

*As Charlotte makes a beeline for her waiting limousine, she's beset by reporters.*

BRIGITTE KLENSCH. *(Chasing after Charlotte.)* Excuse me — Frau von Mahlsdorf — Brigitte Klensch, journalist, Berlin. You say you murdered your father. Has anyone inquired after his death certificate? Court records from your trial?
CHARLOTTE. Pardon me, please. *Mein Auto* — the driver, he is waiting —
BRIGITTE KLENSCH. To date, I've found nothing to confirm your claims —
CHARLOTTE. *(Evasively:)* In the war, such records, they were lost, yes? — flying through the air like burning leaves —
KARL HENNING. Charlotte! Karl Henning, from Munich. Isn't it true that the Stasi hired you to appraise furniture?
CHARLOTTE. I remember 1945 like it was only yesterday, but if you ask me, "What did you have for breakfast?" I don't know!
KARL HENNING. According to records we've obtained, you valued furnishings torn from the homes of dissidents, of political prisoners, of the wronged and the oppressed —
CHARLOTTE. You are from the West, yes? Did the Stasi ever come to your door? Tell me, I ask you — !
FRANCOIS GARNIER. Francois Garnier, Paris. Did the Stasi really pay you in contraband?

CHARLOTTE. I took nothing!

FRANCOIS GARNIER. — not even an inkwell, a cigarette box for your museum —

CHARLOTTE. *(Vehemently.)* As a mother would take an orphan child, yes?

SHIRLEY BLACKER. *(Very Brooklyn.)* Shirley Blacker, New York City. Why do you suppose the public accepted your story with so little scrutiny?

CHARLOTTE. Please! I am old — so old — *I am tired* —

DAISUKE YAMAGISHI. Daisuke Yamagishi, Tokyo. Is it true your family considers you a public embarrassment? That even your own brother refutes your claims?

MARK FINLEY. *(Gay activist.)* Mark Finley, San Francisco. We — as homosexuals — have been systematically denied our own history. Our own past. Perhaps that's why we're so eager to embrace a martyr, even when she's made of glass?

PRADEEP GUPTA. Pradeep Gupta, Bombay. Is it true that you're really a woman after all?

CLIVE TWIMBLEY. *(A heated East Ender.)* Clive Twimbley, London. Did you know that the very man responsible for your medal recently told this newspaper — and I quote — "Whenever Charlotte von Mahlsdorf opens her mouth to yawn, she's already begun to lie." *(Charlotte pauses, stunned, more accustomed to adoration than such vicious censure. She turns to the throng, and says with quiet intensity, as a balm to soothe herself.)*

CHARLOTTE. When I was almost forty years old, my mother was doing the laundry, yes? Hanging my stockings and my garters on the line. And she turned to me, and she said, "Lottchen, it's all very well to play dress-up. But now you've grown into a man. When will you marry?" *(She raises her eyes to look at them each in turn.)* And I said to her, "Never, my dear Mutti. *Ich bin meine eigene Frau.* I am my own wife." *(A psychiatrist steps forward to "settle" the matter with science.)*

## SUPERTITLE: DIAGNOSIS

DIETER JORGENSEN. Dieter Jorgensen, psychiatrist, Bonn.

Berlin's most notorious transvestite is neither a raconteur nor Machiavellian; she is, in fact, mentally ill. Charlotte von Mahlsdorf suffers from autism.

43

Listen to the manner in which she recounts her stories: in a highly ritualized, cadenced way, less to communicate content than to provide a kind of rhythmic reassurance to the chaos in her psyche. This is true of autistic adults; repetition is a palliative. Her stories aren't lies per se; they're self-medication.

## SUPERTITLE: ON CURATING

*We join Doug in the middle of an impassioned, climactic argument with John Marks.*

DOUG. So — at the end of the day — what have I got? A shoe-box full of scratchy audiotapes. A used copy of *Die Transvestiten*. Enormous personal bias. Not to mention, my German *sucks* —
JOHN. I say, you go with what's in plain, old-fashioned black-and-white. The press reports, the file —
DOUG. But I need to believe in her stories as much as she does! I need to believe that — a long time ago, in an attic — a generous aunt handed her confused nephew a book and a blessing. That a little boy — *in his mother's house-coat* — survived *Storm Troopers*. That Lothar Berfelde navigated a path between the two most repressive regimes the Western World has ever known — the *Nazis* and the *Communists* — in a pair of heels.

I need to believe that things like that are true. That they can happen in the world.
JOHN. So what're you gonna do?
DOUG. I don't have a clue. I'm curating her now, and I don't have the faintest idea what to edit, and what to preserve. *(Suddenly, from the recesses of the past, an idea. A memory of something said.)* Tape Eight … March 4, 1993 … *(Doug turns to Charlotte to proffer a query:)* Charlotte, what do you do when a piece loses its luster? Are you ever tempted to strip the wood, or replace the veneer?
CHARLOTTE. I did not refinish the pieces. No. *Diese alte Anrichte?* The polish is as old as the object itself. It is antique, too. *(Charlotte approaches the miniature museum; she takes out the large, velvet-lined box. She picks up the tiny vertiko.)* Nicks and cuts. Stains. Cracks. *(She places it tenderly in the box. Next, a tiny sideboard.)* A missing balustrade; a broken spindle. These things, they are proof of its

history. And so you must leave it. *(She places it snugly in the box, too. Then the small sofa; the doll-sized chair.)* The furniture in my museum is more than one century old. People sat on it, slept on it, wrote letters on it, ate from it. *(She tucks away the kitchen contraption.)* People tried to burn it. In Nazi times. In Stasi times. *(The bust of Kaiser Wilhelm II. The regulator.)* And still, it is standing. It was not only decoration. It was used. *(Doug passes a diminutive phonograph to her.)*

DOUG. Does a piece ever get so old — so damaged — that you throw it away? *(She takes it from him and places it in the box, too.)*

CHARLOTTE. Nein. You must save everything. And you must show it — *auf Englisch* we say — "as is." *(She closes the lid with finality.)* It is a record, yes? Of living. Of lives. *(Charlotte removes her kerchief and becomes Doug. As he speaks, Doug unclasps Charlotte's pearls from around his neck. He places them gently top the furniture box.)*

DOUG. Charlotte von Mahlsdorf did, in fact, move to Sweden, where she lived for almost seven years. But in April of 2002, she decided to take a holiday, to fly back to Berlin, a homecoming of sorts. While visiting her beloved Grunderzeit Museum, she suffered a heart attack. Alone in a garden of gramophone horns, she died.

A few days after her funeral, an envelope arrived in my mailbox; I recognized her familiar script. But no letter. Instead, she'd enclosed a single photograph, sepia with age.

In it, she's a child. A boy. Lothar Berfelde, at ten years old.

## SUPERTITLE: BETWEEN TWO LIONS

*Doug crosses center, entering a pool of light.*

DOUG. He's at the zoo in Berlin. He's wearing a sailor suit, with a blue collar and matching cuffs. His ears are sticking out at an angle; he's got a very adorable smile. He's on a bench.

Sitting on either side of him, two lions. Cubs, sure, but they're still as big as he is. And they're not fond of posing, either. Their eyes are dangerously alert. At any moment they might revolt; they might scratch, or bite. *(He says with awe:)* But Lothar has one arm around each lion, and they're resting their forepaws on his knees. *(Doug walks to the phonograph, and places the needle on the wax cylinder.*

*Through its horn, the sound of an original, taped interview with Charlotte von Mahlsdorf, made in 1993 on a scratchy micro-cassette. The sound quality is poor, but the words are intelligible.)*

TAPE RECORDING.    *(The voice of Doug:)* Tape Four with Charlotte von Mahlsdorf, February 2nd, 1993. I'm on the way to Mahlsdorf to meet with her now. *(A soft click as the tape recorder is turned off, then on again. The voice of Charlotte:)* Now this is the first room of the museum. And this here is a little phonograph, and on this record you see the picture of Thomas Alva Edison. And he was the inventor of the first talking machine of the world in July of 1877. And the record is made by the National Phonograph Company in Orange, New Jersey. *(On the recording, we hear Charlotte place the needle on the Edison wax roll. The needle idles a moment, then we hear the tinny, glorious sound of an old-fashioned waltz. Doug stands, listening. Fade out.)*

## End of Play

# PROPERTY LIST

Antique Edison phonograph
Mini tape recorder
Phonograph needle
Velvet jewelry box containing miniature furniture
Small collection box
Letter
Book
Edison Amberol
Small guidebook, *Berlin von Hinten*
Slip of paper
Newspaper clippings
Eyeglasses
Cigarette

# SOUND EFFECTS

Old German waltz
Music from an Edison Amberol
"Sound of nostalgia"
Short tones of a European phone ringing
Answering machine
Pompous music
Applause
Cheers
German disco song
Sounds of an old pianola
Slam of a prison door
Ticking of an enormous clock
Ear-piercing gong of a clock striking midnight
Sound of old music boxes
Broadcast news music
Euro-Pop music
Laughter
Voice of Charlotte von Mahlsdorf

# NEW PLAYS

★ **MONTHS ON END by Craig Pospisil.** In comic scenes, one for each month of the year, we follow the intertwined worlds of a circle of friends and family whose lives are poised between happiness and heartbreak. "...a triumph...these twelve vignettes all form crucial pieces in the eternal puzzle known as human relationships, an area in which the playwright displays an assured knowledge that spans deep sorrow to unbounded happiness." –*Ann Arbor News.* "...rings with emotional truth, humor...[an] endearing contemplation on love...entertaining and satisfying." –*Oakland Press.* [5M, 5W] ISBN: 0-8222-1892-5

★ **GOOD THING by Jessica Goldberg.** Brings us into the households of John and Nancy Roy, forty-something high-school guidance counselors whose marriage has been increasingly on the rocks and Dean and Mary, recent graduates struggling to make their way in life. "...a blend of gritty social drama, poetic humor and unsubtle existential contemplation..." –*Variety.* [3M, 3W] ISBN: 0-8222-1869-0

★ **THE DEAD EYE BOY by Angus MacLachlan.** Having fallen in love at their Narcotics Anonymous meeting, Billy and Shirley-Diane are striving to overcome the past together. But their relationship is complicated by the presence of Sorin, Shirley-Diane's fourteen-year-old son, a damaged reminder of her dark past. "...a grim, insightful portrait of an unmoored family..." –*NY Times.* "MacLachlan's play isn't for the squeamish, but then, tragic stories delivered at such an unrelenting fever pitch rarely are." –*Variety.* [1M, 1W, 1 boy] ISBN: 0-8222-1844-5

★ **[SIC] by Melissa James Gibson.** In adjacent apartments three young, ambitious neighbors come together to discuss, flirt, argue, share their dreams and plan their futures with unequal degrees of deep hopefulness and abject despair. "A work...concerned with the sound and power of language..." –*NY Times.* "...a wonderfully original take on urban friendship and the comedy of manners—a *Design for Living* for our times..." –*NY Observer.* [3M, 2W] ISBN: 0-8222-1872-0

★ **LOOKING FOR NORMAL by Jane Anderson.** Roy and Irma's twenty-five-year marriage is thrown into turmoil when Roy confesses that he is actually a woman trapped in a man's body, forcing the couple to wrestle with the meaning of their marriage and the delicate dynamics of family. "Jane Anderson's bittersweet transgender domestic comedy-drama ...is thoughtful and touching and full of wit and wisdom. A real audience pleaser." –*Hollywood Reporter.* [5M, 4W] ISBN: 0-8222-1857-7

★ **ENDPAPERS by Thomas McCormack.** The regal Joshua Maynard, the old and ailing head of a mid-sized, family-owned book-publishing house in New York City, must name a successor. One faction in the house backs a smart, "pragmatic" manager, the other faction a smart, "sensitive" editor and both factions fear what the other's man could do to this house— and to them. "If Kaufman and Hart had undertaken a comedy about the publishing business, they might have written *Endpapers*...a breathlessly fast, funny, and thoughtful comedy ...keeps you amused, guessing, and often surprised...profound in its empathy for the paradoxes of human nature." –*NY Magazine.* [7M, 4W] ISBN: 0-8222-1908-5

★ **THE PAVILION by Craig Wright.** By turns poetic and comic, romantic and philosophical, this play asks old lovers to face the consequences of difficult choices made long ago. "The script's greatest strength lies in the genuineness of its feeling." –*Houston Chronicle.* "Wright's perceptive, gently witty writing makes this familiar situation fresh and thoroughly involving." –*Philadelphia Inquirer.* [2M, 1W (flexible casting)] ISBN: 0-8222-1898-4

**DRAMATISTS PLAY SERVICE, INC.**
440 Park Avenue South, New York, NY 10016  212-683-8960  Fax 212-213-1539
postmaster@dramatists.com  www.dramatists.com

# NEW PLAYS

★ **BE AGGRESSIVE by Annie Weisman.** Vista Del Sol is paradise, sandy beaches, avocado-lined streets. But for seventeen-year-old cheerleader Laura, everything changes when her mother is killed in a car crash, and she embarks on a journey to the Spirit Institute of the South where she can learn "cheer" with Bible belt intensity. "...filled with lingual gymnastics...stylized rapid-fire dialogue..." *–Variety.* "...a new, exciting, and unique voice in the American theatre..." *–BackStage West.* [1M, 4W, extras] ISBN: 0-8222-1894-1

★ **FOUR by Christopher Shinn.** Four people struggle desperately to connect in this quiet, sophisticated, moving drama. "...smart, broken-hearted...Mr. Shinn has a precocious and forgiving sense of how power shifts in the game of sexual pursuit...He promises to be a playwright to reckon with..." *–NY Times.* "A voice emerges from an American place. It's got humor, sadness and a fresh and touching rhythm that tell of the loneliness and secrets of life...[a] poetic, haunting play." *–NY Post.* [3M, 1W] ISBN: 0-8222-1850-X

★ **WONDER OF THE WORLD by David Lindsay-Abaire.** A madcap picaresque involving Niagara Falls, a lonely tour-boat captain, a pair of bickering private detectives and a husband's dirty little secret. "Exceedingly whimsical and playfully wicked. Winning and genial. A top-drawer production." *–NY Times.* "Full frontal lunacy is on display. A most assuredly fresh and hilarious tragicomedy of marital discord run amok...absolutely hysterical..." *–Variety.* [3M, 4W (doubling)] ISBN: 0-8222-1863-1

★ **QED by Peter Parnell.** Nobel Prize-winning physicist and all-around genius Richard Feynman holds forth with captivating wit and wisdom in this fascinating biographical play that originally starred Alan Alda. "QED is a seductive mix of science, human affections, moral courage, and comic eccentricity. It reflects on, among other things, death, the absence of God, travel to an unexplored country, the pleasures of drumming, and the need to know and understand." *–NY Magazine.* "Its rhythms correspond to the way that people—even geniuses—approach and avoid highly emotional issues, and it portrays Feynman with affection and awe." *–The New Yorker.* [1M, 1W] ISBN: 0-8222-1924-7

★ **UNWRAP YOUR CANDY by Doug Wright.** Alternately chilling and hilarious, this deliciously macabre collection of four bedtime tales for adults is guaranteed to keep you awake for nights on end. "Engaging and intellectually satisfying...a treat to watch." *–NY Times.* "Fiendishly clever. Mordantly funny and chilling. Doug Wright teases, freezes and zaps us." *–Village Voice.* "Four bite-size plays that bite back." *–Variety.* [flexible casting] ISBN: 0-8222-1871-2

★ **FURTHER THAN THE FURTHEST THING by Zinnie Harris.** On a remote island in the middle of the Atlantic secrets are buried. When the outside world comes calling, the islanders find their world blown apart from the inside as well as beyond. "Harris winningly produces an intimate and poetic, as well as political, family saga." *–Independent (London).* "Harris' enthralling adventure of a play marks a departure from stale, well-furrowed theatrical terrain." *–Evening Standard (London).* [3M, 2W] ISBN: 0-8222-1874-7

★ **THE DESIGNATED MOURNER by Wallace Shawn.** The story of three people living in a country where what sort of books people like to read and how they choose to amuse themselves becomes both firmly personal and unexpectedly entangled with questions of survival. "This is a playwright who does not just tell you what it is like to be arrested at night by goons or to fall morally apart and become an aimless yet weirdly contented ghost yourself. He has the originality to make you feel it." *–Times (London).* "A fascinating play with beautiful passages of writing..." *–Variety.* [2M, 1W] ISBN: 0-8222-1848-8

**DRAMATISTS PLAY SERVICE, INC.**
440 Park Avenue South, New York, NY 10016  212-683-8960  Fax 212-213-1539
postmaster@dramatists.com  www.dramatists.com

# NEW PLAYS

★ **SHEL'S SHORTS by Shel Silverstein.** Lauded poet, songwriter and author of children's books, the incomparable Shel Silverstein's short plays are deeply infused with the same wicked sense of humor that made him famous. "…[a] childlike honesty and twisted sense of humor." –*Boston Herald.* "…terse dialogue and an absurdity laced with a tang of dread give [*Shel's Shorts*] more than a trace of Samuel Beckett's comic existentialism." –*Boston Phoenix.* [flexible casting] ISBN: 0-8222-1897-6

★ **AN ADULT EVENING OF SHEL SILVERSTEIN by Shel Silverstein.** Welcome to the darkly comic world of Shel Silverstein, a world where nothing is as it seems and where the most innocent conversation can turn menacing in an instant. These ten imaginative plays vary widely in content, but the style is unmistakable. "…[*An Adult Evening*] shows off Silverstein's virtuosic gift for wordplay…[and] sends the audience out…with a clear appreciation of human nature as perverse and laughable." –*NY Times.* [flexible casting] ISBN: 0-8222-1873-9

★ **WHERE'S MY MONEY? by John Patrick Shanley.** A caustic and sardonic vivisection of the institution of marriage, laced with the author's inimitable razor-sharp wit. "…Shanley's gift for acid-laced one-liners and emotionally tumescent exchanges is certainly potent…" –*Variety.* "…lively, smart, occasionally scary and rich in reverse wisdom." –*NY Times.* [3M, 3W] ISBN: 0-8222-1865-8

★ **A FEW STOUT INDIVIDUALS by John Guare.** A wonderfully screwy comedy-drama that figures Ulysses S. Grant in the throes of writing his memoirs, surrounded by a cast of fantastical characters, including the Emperor and Empress of Japan, the opera star Adelina Patti and Mark Twain. "Guare's smarts, passion and creativity skyrocket to awesome heights…" –*Star Ledger.* "…precisely the kind of good new play that you might call an everyday miracle…every minute of it is fresh and newly alive…" –*Village Voice.* [10M, 3W] ISBN: 0-8222-1907-7

★ **BREATH, BOOM by Kia Corthron.** A look at fourteen years in the life of Prix, a Bronx native, from her ruthless girl-gang leadership at sixteen through her coming to maturity at thirty. "…vivid world, believable and eye-opening, a place worthy of a dramatic visit, where no one would want to live but many have to." –*NY Times.* "…rich with humor, terse vernacular strength and gritty detail…" –*Variety.* [1M, 9W] ISBN: 0-8222-1849-6

★ **THE LATE HENRY MOSS by Sam Shepard.** Two antagonistic brothers, Ray and Earl, are brought together after their father, Henry Moss, is found dead in his seedy New Mexico home in this classic Shepard tale. "…His singular gift has been for building mysteries out of the ordinary ingredients of American family life…" –*NY Times.* "…rich moments …Shepard finds gold." –*LA Times.* [7M, 1W] ISBN: 0-8222-1858-5

★ **THE CARPETBAGGER'S CHILDREN by Horton Foote.** One family's history spanning from the Civil War to WWII is recounted by three sisters in evocative, intertwining monologues. "…bittersweet music—[a] rhapsody of ambivalence…in its modest, garrulous way…theatrically daring." –*The New Yorker.* [3W] ISBN: 0-8222-1843-7

★ **THE NINA VARIATIONS by Steven Dietz.** In this funny, fierce and heartbreaking homage to *The Seagull*, Dietz puts Chekhov's star-crossed lovers in a room and doesn't let them out. "A perfect little jewel of a play…" –*Shepherdstown Chronicle.* "…a delightful revelation of a writer at play; and also an odd, haunting, moving theater piece of lingering beauty." –*Eastside Journal (Seattle).* [1M, 1W (flexible casting)] ISBN: 0-8222-1891-7

**DRAMATISTS PLAY SERVICE, INC.**
440 Park Avenue South, New York, NY 10016  212-683-8960  Fax 212-213-1539
postmaster@dramatists.com  www.dramatists.com